Sisters at the Beach

Written by Carol Haver, Diana Smith, and Karen Jacobs
Illustrated by Diana Smith

Copyright © 2016 by Karen Jacobs

ISBN: 978-0-9850440-5-3

No part of this book may be reproduced or transmitted in any form or by any means, electronic or mechanical, including photocopying, recording or by any information storage and retrieval system, without written permission from the author, except for the inclusion of brief quotations in reviews.

First edition 2016

Printed in the United States of America

This book is dedicated to all kids with disabilities and their siblings, especially my own sisters. I hope this story shows you how much you mean to me, and that this dedication makes you more willing to let me borrow your clothes.

I love you.

C.H.

My name is Liz, and I'm six-and-a-half years old.

I have a big sister named Jeanie. She is nine, almost ten.

Jeanie has to use a **wheelchair** because she cannot walk.
Her left leg is not as strong as her right leg,
and her left arm is not as strong as her right arm.

Jeanie doesn't talk too much either, but she sure does smile a lot! Jeanie always lets you know if she is happy or sad.

Most of the time, Jeanie is happy.

4

Jeanie is a bit different than some girls, but that does not stop her from being a great sister.

She plays dolls with me,

and we even build castles together.

Today, Mom and Dad are taking us to the beach!

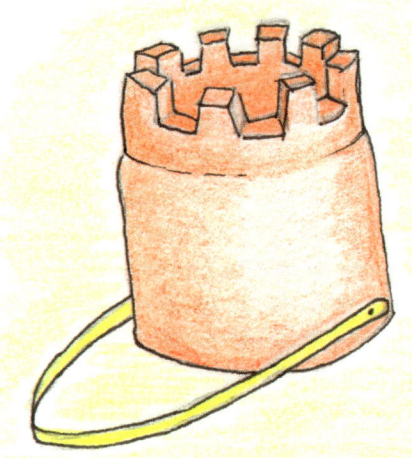

We pack our sand toys,

a cooler,

the sunscreen,

a beach umbrella,

beach chairs,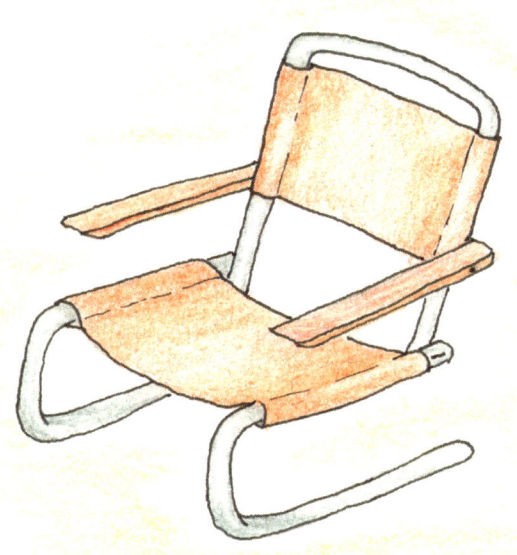

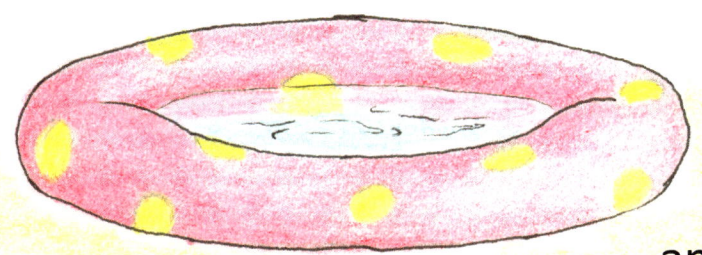

and Jeanie's toys and kiddie pool.

Then we head down the **ramp** to the beach!

"Oh look!" I say.

"There's my friend Tina and her big sister Michelle!"

We set up our chairs beside them.

"Why is your sister sitting in that funny looking chair?" Tina asks me.

"Jeanie needs this chair to help her move around on the sand." I tell Tina.

"We like to explore the beach together."

"We like to go for walks, too!" says Michelle.

I take out the **special paddle** that Jeanie uses to play catch.
We toss a ball back and forth.

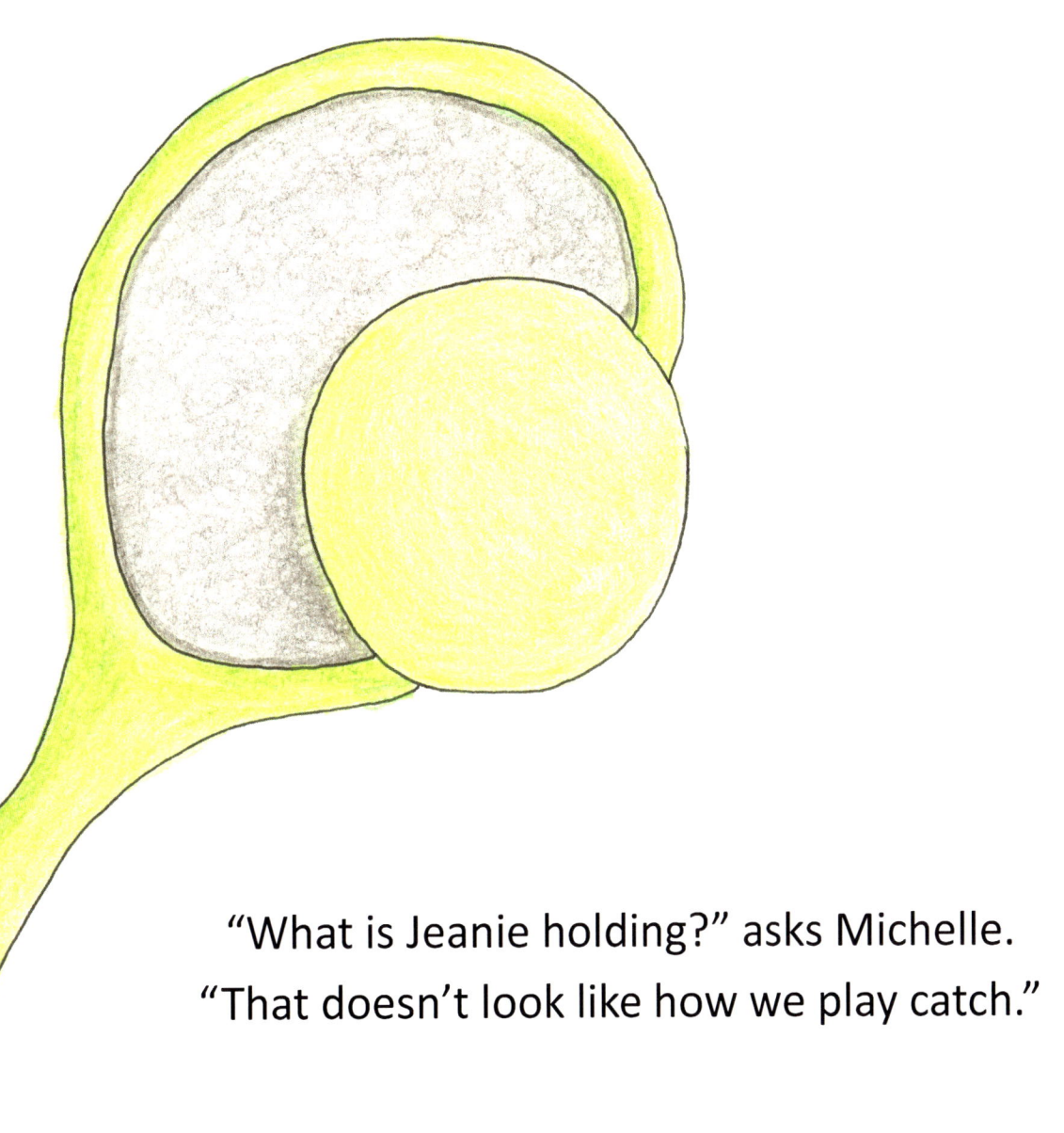

"What is Jeanie holding?" asks Michelle.
"That doesn't look like how we play catch."

"Jeanie's **occupational therapist** showed us how she can play catch with only one hand." I explain.

"She hardly ever drops the ball now!"

Michelle drops her ball on the ground by accident.

"I sure could use a paddle like that!" she laughs.

I go to the cooler to get some snacks.
I take a juice box for me and a **sippy-cup** for Jeanie.

We eat grapes and drink our juice together.

Tina and Michelle drink out of water bottles.

"Jeanie is as old as Michelle." Tina says.
"Why does she use a sippy-cup?"

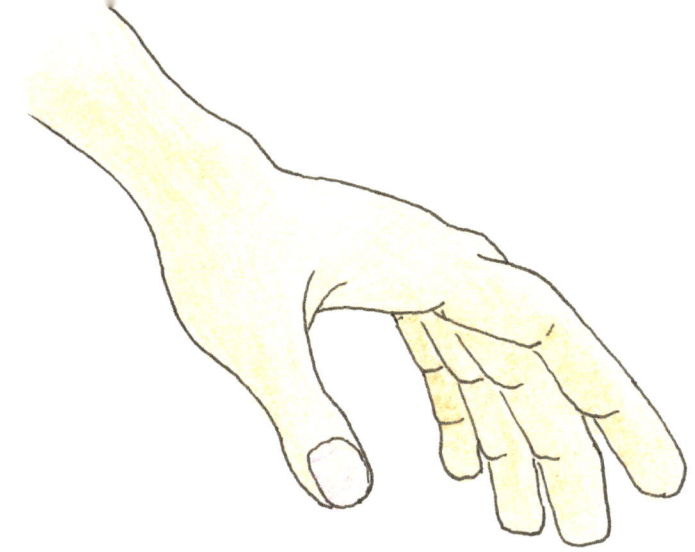
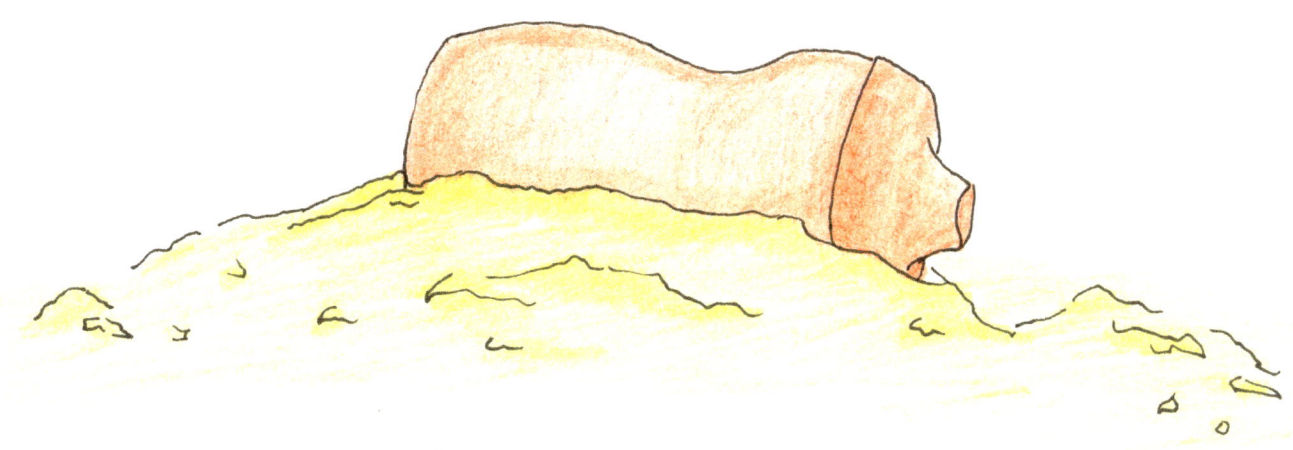

Jeanie drops her cup on the sand, and because it is a sippy-cup her juice doesn't spill.

She picks it up and just keeps drinking!

"Oh cool!" Tina and Michelle say together.

I can tell they are starting
to understand Jeanie just like I do.

It gets very hot outside. We decide to go for a swim in the ocean.

Jeanie and I sit at the edge
of the water so the waves can splash our legs.

Tina and Michelle swim far out in the water,
so I ask if they want to play with me and Jeanie.

They swim over to us.

Jeanie splashes Tina. Michelle splashes me!

We all play in the ocean together.

It's time to build a sandcastle!

Jeanie digs a hole for sand. Tina puts the sand into a bucket.

I flip the bucket over. And Michelle lifts it up!

"What a lovely castle!" says my mom.

"Let me take a picture of these four sisters playing together."

In this story, you met a girl named Jeanie. Jeanie cannot walk or talk, but she still loves to play with her sister Liz! She uses some adapted tools to help her do the things she enjoys, like going to the beach.

An **adaptation** is a change to an activity that makes it easier to do. You can change what you do, how you do it, or the tools that you use. make an activity easier.

Jeanie's **beach wheelchair** is an adaptation because the big rubber wheels help her move around on the sand.

Jeanie's **special paddle** has Velcro® that helps the ball stick to it. This paddle lets Jeanie play catch using only one hand!

An **occupational therapist** is a person who helps you to do things you want and need to do. Jeanie's occupational therapist helped her with adaptations so she could play on the beach with Liz, Tina, and Michelle.

Adaptations might look different compared to how many people do an activity. The important thing to remember is that people who use adaptations can still do the same things as people who do not use them. That is what makes adaptations so cool!

About Us

Carol Haver is number three of the four sisters who inspired *Sisters at the Beach*. She is originally from North Carolina, but moved to Boston to study occupational therapy at Boston University. Carol is incredibly grateful for the people she has met and the opportunities presented to her in this wonderful city. When not at the beach with her family, Carol loves to read, write, and dance.

Karen Jacobs is an occupational therapist and an ergonomist. She is a Clinical Professor in Department of Occupational Therapy at the College of Health & Rehabilitation Sciences: Sargent College at Boston University. She is the proud mother of three children: Laela, Josh, and Ariel; and Amma (grandma in Icelandic) to Sophie, Zachary, Liberty, and Zane. She loves to spend time with her family at Wakonda Pond in Moultonborough, New Hampshire. This is Karen's 6th co-authored children's book (*How Full is Sophia's Backpack, Three Bakers & a Loon, All Paws In, Otter Awesome, & Soaring with Jimmy*). You can reach Karen at kjacobs@bu.edu.

Diana Smith grew up in the Hudson Valley of New York hiking the Gunks and the Bear Mountain. She also enjoys drawing and painting in her free time but found creating the illustrations for this book to be especially meaningful due to its simple and yet powerful message. She is excited to enter practice as an occupational therapist soon and bring the message of this book with her.

CPSIA information can be obtained
at www.ICGtesting.com
Printed in the USA
LVIC06n1211180818
587204LV00002B/15